SPECIAL
CEREMONIES

Weddings

Cath Senker

WAYLAND

SPECIAL CEREMONIES
Weddings

This book is based on the original title *Weddings* by Linda Sonntag, in the *Ceremonies and Celebrations* series, published in 2000 by Hodder Wayland

This differentiated text version is by Cath Senker, published in Great Britain in 2005 by Hodder Wayland, an imprint of Hodder Children's Books.

This paperback edition published in 2006 by Wayland, an imprint of Hachette Children's Books.

Reprinted in 2007

Original designer: Tim Mayer
Layout for this edition: Jane Hawkins

Consultants:
Working Group on Sikhs and Education (WORKSE);
Rasamandala Das;
Jane Clements, The Council of Christians and Jews;
Jonathan Gorsky, The Council of Christians and Jews;
Dr Fatma Amer, The London Central Mosque;
The Clear Vision Trust.

Picture acknowledgements: Circa Picture Library 10 (Ged Murray), 11 (Barrie Searle), 12 (Ged Murray), 28 (John Smith); Hutchison Library 1, 4, 6, 8 (Robert Francis), 9 (Nancy Durrell McKenna), 13 (Liba Taylor), 14 (R. Aberman), 16, 19 (K. Rodgers), 21 (John Hatt), 22 (M. MacIntyre), 26 (Liba Taylor), 29; Panos Pictures 5, 7, 15 (John Miles), 17 (Mark McEvoy), 18, 20 (Leo Dugust), 23 (Dean Chapman), 24 (Paul Cluagle), 25 (Leo Dugust), 27 (Liba Taylor).

British Library Cataloguing in Publication Data
Senker, Cath
Weddings. - Juvenile literature 2. Marriage - Religious aspects - Juvenile literature
I. Title II. Sonntag, Linda, 1950-
203.8'5

ISBN-13: 978 0 7502 4974 4

Printed in China

Wayland
An imprint of Hachette Children's Books
338 Euston Road, London NW1 3BH

Contents

Why do People Get Married?

People get married because they love each other and want to care for one another. They probably want to raise children, and teach them the customs and traditions of their religion. It takes a lot of commitment to get married. The couple will need to work hard to support each other through both the good and bad times.

For people of many religions around the world, it is important to have a ceremony according to their religious traditions.

WEDDING RINGS

A man and woman often exchange rings during the wedding ceremony. The ring stands for the bond between the two people. A ring shows that a person is committed to his or her partner.

The custom of throwing confetti over the bride and groom comes from Italy. ▶

The wedding day is an occasion for great celebration. Friends and family come to the ceremony, bringing gifts. Usually there is a wedding feast and a big party afterwards. People of different faiths have many kinds of marriage ceremonies.

This Russian bride and bridegroom will have their photo taken in front of the cathedral. ▼

The Christian Tradition

Around the world, many Christian couples get married in a church. They vow to love and care for each other for the rest of their lives. People who don't usually go to church can get married at a register office.

Getting engaged

When two people decide to get married, they often get engaged. The man may give the woman an engagement ring. If they are Protestants, the vicar may call banns in church. For three weeks running, he reads out their names. If the congregation know of any reason why the couple should not marry, they can say so.

▲ A few days before the wedding, the bride may have a 'hen night' – a party with her female friends.

Having children is important to many Christians. The Christian holy book, the Bible, mentions it many times. One of the reasons why couples get married is to have children.

The two families work hard to prepare for the wedding. They send invitations to relatives and friends. They also choose a wedding cake, special food, clothes, music and flowers for the big day.

▲ The bride often has a beautiful wedding dress specially made for her.

HOLY BOOK

'Love is always patient and kind. It envies no one. Love is never boastful or conceited [too proud]. It is never rude or quick to take offence. Love does not keep score of wrongs. It does not gloat over other people's misfortunes but delights in the truth.'

From *The Bible: 1 Corinthians 13: 4–7*

A traditional church wedding

The groom stands near the altar with his best man. With music playing, the bride walks up the aisle, usually with her father. Many brides wear a white dress, and have bridesmaids to hold the long train.

The service

The couple repeat their vows after the vicar and exchange rings. Everyone sings hymns and there are Bible readings. Finally, the bride and bridegroom sign the register. As they leave the church, people throw confetti or rice over them for good luck.

◄ This couple are getting married outdoors.

▲ Here the bride and groom sign the register.

The wedding feast

At the feast, the bride's father, the groom and the best man make speeches. Everyone drinks to the bride and groom's happiness, and they cut the wedding cake together. Then it is time for music and dancing.

The honeymoon

The couple leave the wedding party, often in a car decorated with balloons. They may go straight off on their honeymoon, a holiday together to begin married life.

ROSIE'S STORY

'I was bridesmaid at my sister's wedding, so I carried her train, the lace headdress trailing from her dress. At the end, my sister threw her flower bouquet into the crowd and I caught it. This is supposed to mean I'll get married next!'

The Jewish Tradition

Jewish people in traditional communities around the world often meet their partner socially. It is up to them to decide if they want to develop a relationship and marry.

Preparing for the wedding

A few days before the big day, the bride goes to a pool called a *mikveh* to purify herself. The groom is sometimes called to read from the *Torah* in the synagogue, on the Sabbath before the ceremony. (The Sabbath runs from sundown on Friday to nightfall on Saturday.)

◄ The groom reads from the *Torah*, the Jewish holy book.

The special day

The wedding day is a happy day. It is also a time for asking forgiveness for past sins. To do this the bride and groom may fast (eat nothing) until after the ceremony.

A rabbi leads the ceremony, which can be in a synagogue, a home, or outdoors. It takes place under the *huppah*, a canopy. It stands for the home they will make together.

The couple, their parents and the rabbi under the *huppah*. ▶

▲ The groom places the veil over his bride's face in the *bedecken* ceremony.

Bedecken

In the *bedecken* ceremony, the groom places the bride's veil over her face. The rabbi recites a blessing as the couple drink from a cup of wine. Then the groom places a ring on the bride's finger.

Breaking the glass

Seven blessings are sung, praising God and wishing the couple happiness. The groom then smashes a glass with his foot. It reminds people of how the Jewish Temple in Jerusalem was destroyed long ago. There is some sadness even in happy moments. Now the guests call out '*Mazel tov!*' (Good luck!).

A week of celebration

The bride and groom sign a marriage contract and then spend a short time alone together. In traditional communities, a whole week of celebrations follows.

At the wedding feast there is singing and dancing. ▼

SACRED TEXT

It is written in the *Talmud*, the Jewish books of law, that:
'A man without a wife is incomplete.'
'All the blessings that a man receives come to him only in the merit of his wife.'

From *The Talmud*

The Muslim Tradition

Muslim families help their adult children to find a suitable partner, usually through friends and relatives. The young people make the final decision themselves. In the *Qur'an* it says that a man may have up to four wives but most Muslim men marry just one.

The marriage contract

Muslims do not have a religious marriage ceremony. Couples make their own legal contract. The husband gives his wife money or property and promises to provide for her. She keeps the possessions she already has.

◀ Men and women in Turkey dancing before a wedding.

After agreeing to marry, the man and woman have an engagement party. They may exchange gold rings. The night before the wedding is Henna Night. In their own homes, the bride and groom have their hands and feet painted with henna paste.

A bride having her hand painted with henna on her Henna Night. ▼

ZAHRA'S STORY

'I live in Iran. When I first met Hasan, we went into a room from opposite doors and gazed at each other in a mirror. The mirror was supposed to show us how we'll look in Paradise.'

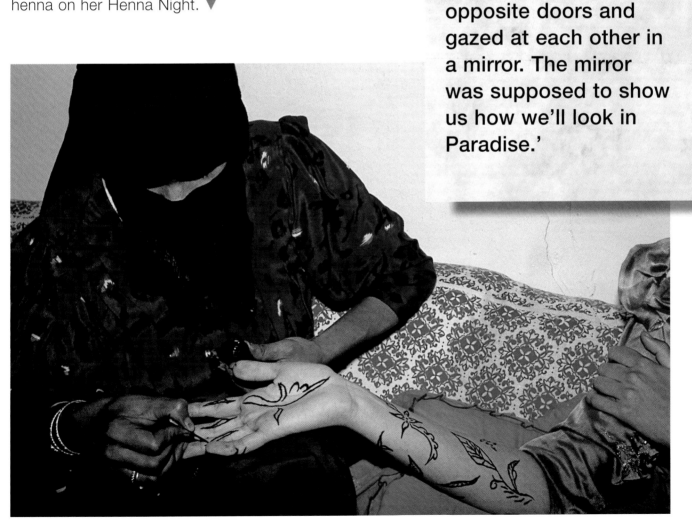

The wedding

Muslims do not have to get married in a mosque. Any Muslim man may marry them. In India or Pakistan, the bride is usually dressed in a red sari, embroidered with gold. The groom wears a white robe or a dark suit. People may place colourful garlands of flowers around his neck.

The bride's sisters and mother go with her to the ceremony. ▼

The bride with her family just before the wedding ceremony. ▶

Husband and wife

The bride and groom sit on opposite sides of the mosque or in different rooms. Two witnesses hear them say their vows. The man leading the wedding reads from the *Qur'an* and talks about the couple's duties. He asks them three times if they agree to be married and then they sign the contract.

Gifts

Now everyone enjoys sweetmeats – nuts, dates and figs. In some countries, the bride's parents hold a party for her friends and family. A week later, the groom gives his own party, the *walima*. At both events, guests bring gifts.

HOLY BOOK

'And among his signs is this, that he created for you mates from among yourselves, that you may dwell in tranquillity [peace] with them, and he has put love and mercy between your hearts.'

From
The Qur'an: 30:21

The Hindu Tradition

Hindu parents may help their children to find a partner. They consult a priest, who reads the couple's horoscopes to check if they are suited. Many young people choose their own partners though. When the engagement is announced, the men and women of both families meet to get to know each other.

A Hindu wedding is usually a big event. The bride may wear several outfits over this time, as well as the red and gold sari she wears for the ceremony.

◀ In India, people may wash in a holy river such as the Ganges to purify themselves before the wedding ceremony.

PADMINI'S STORY

'I live in Canada. My wedding feast was in a beautiful garden. We ate curry with real gold flakes in it to bring good fortune. Twenty chefs made food for all our guests. The wedding lasted for hours. By the end of the day I was very tired, but it was fantastic!'

A sacred place

The wedding is often held in a hall or a wedding garden. A sacred place is set up with a decorated canopy. The bride hides out of sight. When the groom enters, lights are waved over his head and grains of rice are thrown to bring good luck and ward off evil. Then his bride comes to greet him.

The groom arrives for the ceremony on horseback. ▼

The ceremony

The bride and groom sit in front of a sacred fire. The priest sprinkles holy water on them and ties their right hands together with a thread that has been blessed. There are prayers and readings, and the pair throw food offerings into the fire.

The seven steps

The priest ties the end of the bride's sari to the groom's scarf to show they are joined together. They walk around the fire together, usually four times. Now the two are married. Then they take seven steps together, making seven wishes. The guests throw flower petals and rice over them and offer gifts.

◀ The bride and groom with the priest. The coconuts stand for the presence of God.

SACRED TEXT

'Take the first step for food, take the second step for strength, the third for prosperity [wealth], the fourth for happiness, the fifth for children. May we have healthy and long-lived sons. Take the sixth step for seasonal pleasures, take the seventh step for friendship.'

From *Ashwalayana Grihya Sutra: The Marriage Mantra*

▲ A Hindu wedding in Bali. The couple wear traditional Balinese clothes.

A new life

After the ceremony, there is a huge feast. Then a procession takes the bride to her new home. She may move in with her husband's family. After the ceremony, there is a huge feast with many courses.

The Buddhist Tradition

At a Buddhist wedding the woman and man agree to live together following the Buddha's teachings about kindness. Buddhist wedding ceremonies vary greatly from one country to another.

Wedding plans

Before the wedding, Japanese Buddhist couples often choose one or two close friends to support them on the day. They decide whether they will dress in Western clothes or traditional dress – such as colourful silk wraps with sashes. Many Buddhists in Japan wear Western clothes for their wedding.

This Japanese bride wears a kimono, the traditional dress of Japan. ▼

TOSHIMOTO'S STORY

'I live in Tokyo. My bride and I dressed in traditional kimonos for our wedding. The ceremony was held at a Shinto shrine in a hotel. We drank rice wine called *saké* and I read out the words of commitment. All our friends were there to watch us being joined together in marriage.'

▲ A wedding in Thailand. The bride's attendants carry sweets and flowers to offer at the shrine to the Buddha.

Weddings at home

In Japan, many Buddhist weddings are in the bride's home. The ceremony is led by a lay leader, a Buddhist who is not a priest. He takes the couple to a holy cabinet that contains a sacred scroll. They perform a ceremony called *Gong-yo*. It involves saying *sutras* (wise sayings from the scriptures) and chanting.

United in marriage

The bride and groom may wear silk bands around their heads, linked by a silk thread. This shows how their minds will be united in marriage. They sip from a small bowl, then a bigger one, and finally an even bigger one. This stands for the way their lives will grow together.

These guests are enjoying a wedding feast in China. ▼

 A couple having their wedding photos taken.

Flowers and rings

The bride and groom make an offering of flowers to the Buddha and may exchange rings. Usually, the leader of the ceremony makes a speech and everyone wishes the couple happiness.

The party

The wedding feast may be in a home, a hall or a restaurant. In Japan, some couples hold a big party with music and laser lights.

SACRED TEXT

'The support of father and mother, the cherishing of wife and children, and peaceful occupations – this is the Highest Blessing.'

From *The Maha-Mangala Sutta: Verse 5 (Buddhist scripture)*

The Sikh Tradition

▲ These women are preparing an elaborate wedding feast.

Sikh parents introduce their children to people they think might make good partners. Once the young people have made their choice, wedding plans are made.

Engagement

The engagement ceremony is at the *gurdwara* (Sikh temple) or at the bride or groom's home. The couple exchange rings and sweetmeats.

POOJA'S STORY

'Nitin and I met through a trusted Sikh website – we used to write each other long emails. We asked our parents to fix our marriage before we even met. It was so exciting when we did meet, two days before our engagement. Our wedding and honeymoon were the most golden days of our lives.'

Wedding celebrations

In India, the groom arrives at the bride's house the day before the wedding and the celebrations last for three days. In the West, the ceremony is usually in the morning and the feast is in the afternoon.

The wedding day starts with the *milni* ceremony. The two families exchange gifts. With male and female guests on opposite sides of the room, the service begins. Generally it is led by a *granthi*, a Sikh priest.

◄ The groom meets his bride wearing this special crown.

◀ The bride wears a bright *shalwar kameez* and the groom wears his best clothes.

Joined with a scarf

The couple sit in front of the holy book, the *Guru Granth Sahib*. There are hymns and prayers, and a talk about the meaning of marriage. Then one end of the groom's scarf is placed in his hand and the other in his bride's hand. The pair make their vows.

The *Lavan*

The *Lavan*, the wedding hymn, is read and sung. After each of the four verses, the couple slowly walk around the holy book. Now they are married and the guests shower them with rose petals. Everyone eats a sweet food called *parshad*.

SACRED TEXT

'In this first circle, God has shown you the duties of family life...Blessed are those who hold God in their hearts. They are always content and happy.'

From *The Lavan: Verse 1*

Starting a new life

Following the ceremony there is a large wedding feast. Well-wishers give money to the couple. Then the groom takes the bride to his home, where she will live with him. She throws a handful of rice over her shoulder in farewell to the guests.

The groom bows before the gifts to thank his guests. ▼

Glossary

aisle the passage down the middle of a church leading to the altar.

altar the holy table at the front of a church.

best man (Christian tradition) a friend of the groom, who supports him at his wedding.

bridesmaid (Christian tradition) a friend of the bride, who supports her at her wedding.

congregation a group of people gathered for worship.

engaged committed to marry someone.

henna a herb that dyes skin or hair red.

holy water water that has been blessed for use in religious acts.

horoscope a description of what is going to happen to someone in the future, depending on the position of the stars and planets when the person was born.

lay a member of a religion who is not a monk, nun or priest.

mosque the place where Muslims meet, pray and study.

offering something that is offered to a god or Buddha as part of a religious ceremony.

Paradise heaven.

parshad a sweet food made from flour, butter and sugar.

priest (Buddhists, Christians, Hindus, Sikhs) a person who performs religious duties.

purify to make clean in a religious way, often before a ceremony.

Qur'an the Muslims' holy book.

rabbi a Jewish religious teacher and leader.

register office a place where legal marriage contracts are made.

sari a long piece of fabric that is wrapped around the body and worn as the main piece of clothing, especially by Indian women.

sin an act that breaks a religious rule.

sweetmeat a food rich in sugar, such as candied fruit (coated with sugar).

vicar a person who works for the Church of England and is in charge of a church.

vow a serious religious promise to do something.

witness someone who watches an important event to make sure it happens as it should.

Books to Read

Beliefs and Cultures: Buddhist; Christian; Hindu; Jewish; Muslim (Watts, 2003)

Eyewitness Books: Judaism by Douglas Charing (Dorling Kindersley, 2003)

The Facts About Buddhism; Sikhism; Judaism; Christianity; Hinduism; Islam by Alison Cooper (Hodder Wayland, 2006)

Life Times: Wedding Days by Anita Ganeri and Jackie Morris (Evans, 1998)

Our Culture: Buddhist; Hindu; Jewish; Muslim; Sikh (Watts, 2003)

Rites of Passage: Weddings by Paul Mason (Heinemann, 2003)

World Book's Celebrations and Rituals Around the World: Marriage Celebrations (World Book Inc., 2003)

A World of Festivals: Life and Death by Jean Coppendale (Chrysalis, 2003)

A Year of Religious Festivals series: *My Buddhist Year; My Christian Year; My Hindu Year; My Jewish Year; My Muslim Year; My Sikh Year;* by Cath Senker (Hodder Wayland, 2004/2005)

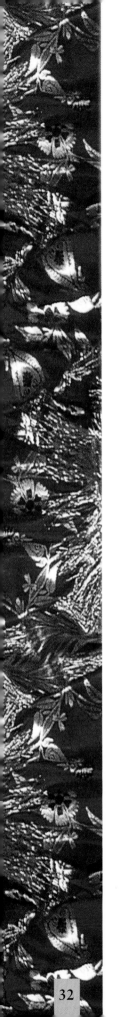

Index

Numbers in **bold** refer to photographs